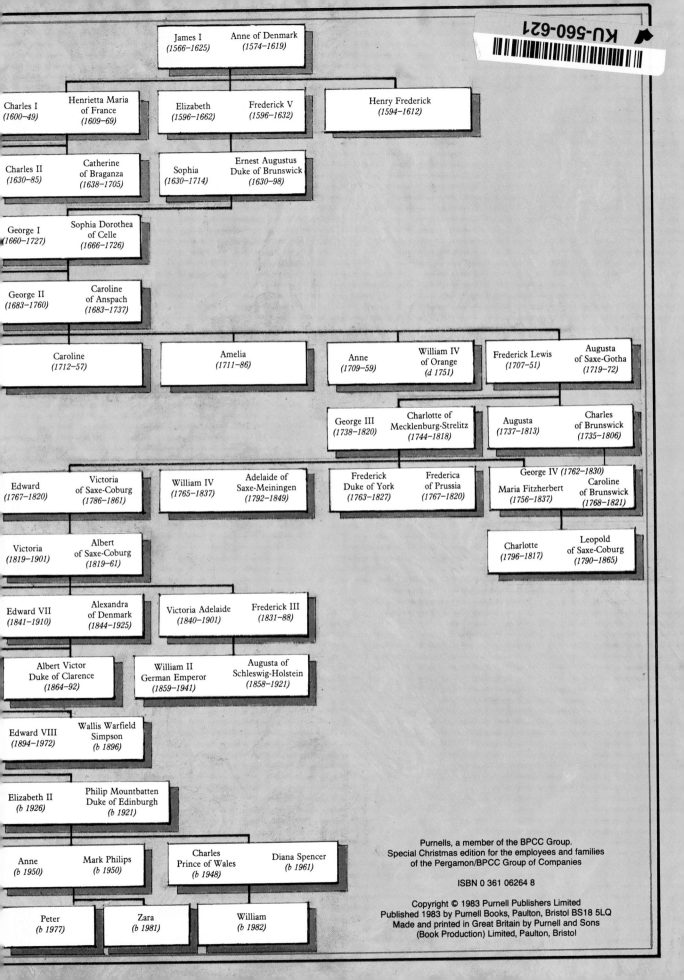

KU-560-621

James I
(1566–1625)

Anne of Denmark
(1574–1619)

Charles I
(1600–49)

Henrietta Maria
of France
(1609–69)

Elizabeth
(1596–1662)

Frederick V
(1596–1632)

Henry Frederick
(1594–1612)

Charles II
(1630–85)

Catherine
of Braganza
(1638–1705)

Sophia
(1630–1714)

Ernest Augustus
Duke of Brunswick
(1630–98)

George I
(1660–1727)

Sophia Dorothea
of Celle
(1666–1726)

George II
(1683–1760)

Caroline
of Anspach
(1683–1737)

Caroline
(1712–57)

Amelia
(1711–86)

Anne
(1709–59)

William IV
of Orange
(d 1751)

Frederick Lewis
(1707–51)

Augusta
of Saxe-Gotha
(1719–72)

George III
(1738–1820)

Charlotte of
Mecklenburg-Strelitz
(1744–1818)

Augusta
(1737–1813)

Charles
of Brunswick
(1735–1806)

Edward
(1767–1820)

Victoria
of Saxe-Coburg
(1786–1861)

William IV
(1765–1837)

Adelaide of
Saxe-Meiningen
(1792–1849)

Frederick
Duke of York
(1763–1827)

Frederica
of Prussia
(1767–1820)

George IV (1762–1830)
Maria Fitzherbert
(1756–1837)

Caroline
of Brunswick
(1768–1821)

Victoria
(1819–1901)

Albert
of Saxe-Coburg
(1819–61)

Charlotte
(1796–1817)

Leopold
of Saxe-Coburg
(1790–1865)

Edward VII
(1841–1910)

Alexandra
of Denmark
(1844–1925)

Victoria Adelaide
(1840–1901)

Frederick III
(1831–88)

Albert Victor
Duke of Clarence
(1864–92)

William II
German Emperor
(1859–1941)

Augusta of
Schleswig-Holstein
(1858–1921)

Edward VIII
(1894–1972)

Wallis Warfield
Simpson
(b 1896)

Elizabeth II
(b 1926)

Philip Mountbatten
Duke of Edinburgh
(b 1921)

Anne
(b 1950)

Mark Philips
(b 1950)

Charles
Prince of Wales
(b 1948)

Diana Spencer
(b 1961)

Peter
(b 1977)

Zara
(b 1981)

William
(b 1982)

Purnells, a member of the BPCC Group.
Special Christmas edition for the employees and families
of the Pergamon/BPCC Group of Companies

ISBN 0 361 06264 8

Copyright © 1983 Purnell Publishers Limited
Published 1983 by Purnell Books, Paulton, Bristol BS18 5LQ
Made and printed in Great Britain by Purnell and Sons
(Book Production) Limited, Paulton, Bristol

FROM ROBERT MAXWELL

**To All Staff, Families and Friends
of the Pergamon/BPCC Group of Companies**

It is my practice each Christmas to send one of the Group's Royal books as a personal gift to each of the many thousand people who give or have given their services to the Pergamon/BPCC Group of Companies in this country and abroad. This is no mere routine gesture; it is a mark of my very real appreciation and respect and that of the Main Boards of the Group of the quality of service and deep loyalty to the Group of so many people.

Last Christmas I referred to the severe challenge of 1982, to the high morale of our management and work people, and to the successes achieved as a result of our combined efforts.

1983 has been another year of challenge - a year of re-equipment, rationalization and reorganization. The foundations of success laid down in 1981/82 have been built upon in 1983. The Group's quite remarkable return to profitability brought immediate benefits to the workforce in increased earnings and job security and will, as from this year's profits, also benefit our shareholders, who will - under our share purchase SAYE scheme - include many of the workforce.

I believe that 1984 will be an exciting year for us all, a year of opportunity, a year of further growth and greater success. Thank you for all your help in the achievements upon which that bright future will be built.

A very joyful Christmas and a happy and peaceful 1984 to all of you and to your families.

Oxford
Christmas 1983

Robert Maxwell
Chairman

Queen Elizabeth II

Brenda Ralph Lewis

Purnell

n 21st April 1926, when Elizabeth Alexandra Mary was born, the first child of the Duke and Duchess of York, no one imagined she was a future Queen of England. That changed, though, when her uncle, King Edward VIII abdicated in 1936 and her father replaced him as King George VI. Till then, Elizabeth and her sister Margaret, born in 1930, had enjoyed a quiet, close family life with their parents. Now, Elizabeth, aged 10, began her training as a future monarch. Her father, whom she loved dearly, played a major part in preparing her for her future role and its duties and responsibilities. On her sixteenth birthday in 1942, Princess Elizabeth received her first official appointment, as Honorary Colonel of the Grenadier Guards. In 1944, at 18, she was granted her own coat of arms, personal standard, official car and her first Lady in Waiting and private secretary. In 1945, the last year of the Second World War, the Princess set an example to other girls of her age by enlisting in the ATS as a junior subaltern.

After the war, she became President of the Red Cross, accompanied her parents on a South African tour and performed royal duties such as launching ships.

At 21, she married Philip Mountbatten, her distant cousin, in a televised ceremony at Westminster Abbey. Prince Philip, Duke of Edinburgh, as he became, was a naval officer and at first, the Princess could live as 'Navy wife'. Soon, though, her father's chronic ill-health obliged her to take on a larger share of royal duty. She was touring Kenya with Philip on 6th February 1952 when King George died and the 25-year-old Princess who had left home only a few days before returned as Queen.

Top left, this picture, showing Elizabeth with her grandmother, Queen Mary, was taken in 1927 to celebrate the Princess's first birthday. She was Queen Mary's favourite grandchild, but sadly, the old Queen died only weeks before Elizabeth's splendid coronation in 1953.
Left, Princess Elizabeth in 1943.

Below, Princess Elizabeth, aged 16 in 1942, is shown here shortly after she became Honorary Colonel of the Grenadier Guards. She wears the regimental badge in her hat. As the military cut of her jacket shows, the Second World War, then in its fourth year, had a distinct effect on fashion. The Princess herself 'joined up' in 1945 to become, at 19, Junior Subaltern No. 230873 in the Auxiliary Territorial Service (ATS) where she became a competent motor mechanic and driver, an unlikely occupation for a royal princess.

Left, the wedding of Princess Elizabeth and Philip Mountbatten on 20th November 1947 was the royal love match the British public had always wanted for her, as well as a joyous, sparkling occasion which brightened the austerity of the years after the Second World War. This picture shows the happy Princess at Buckingham Palace, shortly before leaving for the Abbey. She wore a wedding dress designed by the royal dressmaker, Norman Hartnell and her wedding ring, like that of the present Princess of Wales, was made of Welsh gold. Princess Margaret, her 17-year-old sister, was chief bridesmaid. The ceremony was televised and watched by millions.

Uniquely, the wedding was watched on television by people all over the world. The year 1947 was eventful for Elizabeth in more ways than one. On her 21st birthday, 21st April, she had broadcast from South Africa, where she was on tour with her parents, vowing that her life would be dedicated to the service of her country. It is a vow she has undoubtedly observed ever since.

The South African tour was meant as a 'test' of the Princess's wish to marry Philip Mountbatten whom she first met, and reportedly fell in love with, when she was only 13. Both of them are great-great grandchildren of Queen Victoria, and the Prince Consort.

Top right, Princess Elizabeth and Prince Philip in a Royal Family group photographed at Buckingham Palace after their wedding. Third on the bride's right is her mother, Queen Elizabeth, with King George VI just behind her. Just to the right behind the bride is Queen Mary, her grandmother. Princess Margaret, the chief bridesmaid, is third on the bride's left.

Left, the royal couple had been married nearly three years when this picture was taken in 1950, with their two elder children: Prince Charles, born on 14th November 1948 and the then new baby, Princess Anne, born at Clarence House on 15th August 1950. Their other children, Prince Andrew and Prince Edward were born in 1960 and 1964.

Above, centre, Queen Elizabeth II in the State Coach after her Coronation at Westminster Abbey on 2nd June 1953. Hers was the first Coronation to be televised. It was also filmed in colour.

Bottom right, Princess Elizabeth, 21, and Prince Philip, 26, in a photograph taken to mark their engagement which was announced on 9th July 1947.

The Public Face

The Queen leads an extremely busy public life. Her many State duties include the distribution of the Royal Maundy at Easter, Trooping the Colour on her official birthday in June, and, in November, the State Opening of Parliament and the Remembrance Service to honour Britain's war dead.

The Queen is kept informed of matters of state by her daily dispatch boxes, and on Tuesdays grants audience to the Prime Minister.

In addition, fourteen investitures are held annually to present awards given in the New Year and Birthday Honours List, and, in 1982 and 1983, the honours and medals won in the Falklands War.

On the social side, the Queen's busy official programme includes the Chelsea Flower Show (May), Ascot Week (June), the Royal Garden Parties (July) and, in December, her televised Christmas broadcast to the nation.

There are also special celebrations (the Queen's Silver Jubilee, 1977, the Queen Mother's 80th Birthday, 1980, the Royal Wedding, 1981), and visits by foreign heads of state, such as Queen Beatrix of the Netherlands and the U.S. President Reagan (1982). The Queen also tours abroad, most recently visiting the West Indies, Mexico, the United States and Sweden.

Left, the Queen wears the Stewart, the official tartan of the Royal Family, at the Ghillies' Ball, in her Silver Wedding year, 1972.

Right, the Queen in Imperial State Crown and Parliamentary Robes in the Buckingham Palace throne room, during her Silver Jubilee year, 1977.

Right, with Prince Philip on her left and the Lords sitting in front of her, the Queen outlines the programme of the Conservative government to both Houses of Parliament, in the House of Lords at the State Opening of Parliament on 26th June 1983.

The investiture of Prince Charles as Prince of Wales took place at Caernarvon Castle on 1st July 1969, when the Queen presented him to the Welsh people. This was only the second time the heir to the English throne had been presented at Caernarvon since the tradition began in 1284. The first was the investiture in 1911 of Prince Edward, later the Duke of Windsor, which was used as a model for the ceremony in 1969. Above, the Queen sits with her son listening to the speeches after the ceremony. Prince Charles himself made a speech in Welsh on this important occasion, which was televised and viewed by millions throughout the world.

Above right, the Queen with the Governor of the Tower of London and the Yeoman Warders, better known as Beefeaters, who wear their colourful 16th-century Tudor costume. In front of them are the ceremonial axe and the partisan, or halberd.

Above far right, 6th February 1977 marked the 25th anniversary of the Queen's accession to the throne. This Silver Jubilee was the first since that of the Queen's grandfather, King George V in 1935. It was marked by celebrations all over Britain and the Commonwealth. In this photograph, the Queen and Prince Philip are seen at the service of thanksgiving in St. Paul's Cathedral, London in June 1977. Below left, the Queen, as Colonel-in-Chief, visits the Argyll and Sutherland Highlanders at their barracks at Catterick. Below right, the Queen, clad in emerald green visits the Emerald Isle. She is seen here after arriving by helicopter at the start of her visit to Belfast in 1977 where a crowd of small children wait to greet her with Union Jacks and flowers. Behind the Queen is the Right Hon Roy Mason M.P., Secretary of State for Northern Ireland in the then Labour government.

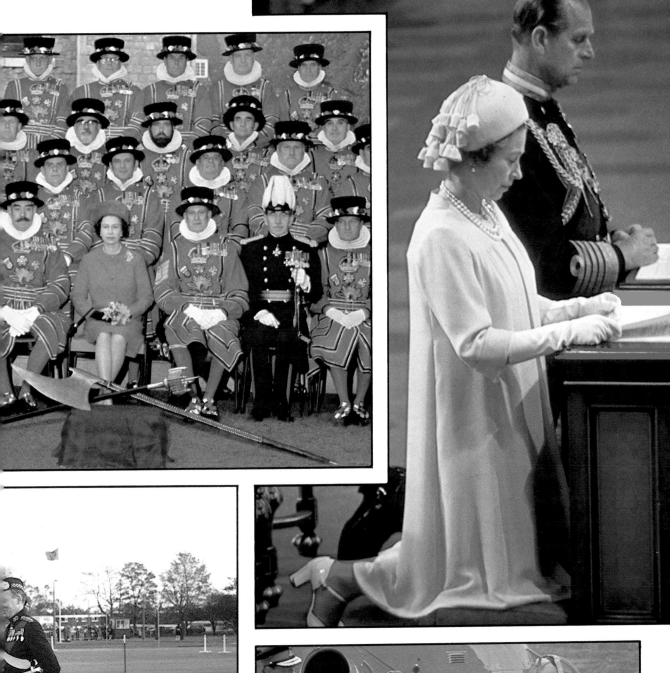

In her Silver Jubilee year, 1977, the Queen visited most parts of Britain. Everywhere, she received heartfelt congratulations. She is seen above left, with Prince Philip and some of the many thousands of floral tributes she was given piled up in the back of their car. Below left, a Royal Jubilee walkabout in dockland: the Queen meets and greets some of the well-wishers who came out in force to see and welcome her. Centre, the Queen at the opera, seen here meeting members of the cast in costume after a performance given in 1976.

Top right, the liner Queen Elizabeth II moves down the slipway at John Brown's Shipyard, Clydebank, after being launched by the Queen on 20th September 1967. Bottom right, lone round-the-world sailor Sir Francis Chichester seen with the Queen at Greenwich. He is about to board his Gypsy Moth IV, which took him on his epic voyage, just after being knighted by the Queen at a public ceremony at the Royal Naval College, Greenwich. This was a replay of the day in 1580 when another Queen Elizabeth, Elizabeth I, knighted another Sir Francis — Drake — after his return from his round-the-world voyage, the first to be achieved by an Englishman.

Every year on 10th June, the Queen's official and Prince Philip's actual birthday, the Brigade of Guards Troop the Colour in Horseguards Parade, behind Whitehall. This is one of London's most colourful royal ceremonies and a splendid military parade with stirring military music which always draws a large of crowd of spectators. Royalty-minded visitors from abroad often time their stay in London to see the Trooping the Colour, which is full of brilliant pageantry. Above, the Queen, riding sidesaddle, takes the salute at the Trooping the Colour. Prince Philip, seen next to her, wears the ceremonial uniform of the Guards, complete with decorations and bearskin. At the Trooping, the Queen reviews the five regiments of Foot Guards and two regiments of mounted Guards.

Above top, the Queen and Prince Philip shown after leaving Buckingham Palace to take part in the Trooping the Colour ceremony. Smiling spectators cram the route despite the rainy weather. Above, the Queen with her youngest son, 8-year-old Prince Edward. The picture was

Trooping the Colour

The midsummer months of June and July are always a busy time for the Queen and her family. In addition to the Trooping the Colour, June also sees the annual service for the six hundred-year-old Order of the Knights of the Garter. The Queen herself is Sovereign of the Order and attends the Service wearing the Order's 'uniform' of plumed hat, long black velvet robes, ribbons and epaulettes. The Service is held at St. George's Chapel, Windsor. On duty there are the Queen's Bodyguard of the Honourable Corps of Gentlemen-at-Arms and the Yeomen of the Guard.

June is also the month when the Queen attends the premier horseracing events of the year: Ascot Week and the Derby at Epsom. Here, royal duties combine happily with the royal passion for horses. At Ascot, the Queen and members of her family ride along the course in open landaus and witness the races that follow with great interest. For the Queen and the Queen Mother, whose love of horses she has inherited, Derby Day at Epsom is a 'must'. The Queen can always be observed watching the event with the same keen and expert eye she beams on the Badminton Horse Trials, another summer date which she keeps regularly.

A series of events of a very different sort takes place in July — the four Royal Garden Parties which are held in the grounds of Buckingham Palace. These Parties replaced the Debutantes' Presentation Parties and Balls and have widened the royals' public social life by including guests from all walks of life. In these busy circumstances, the Royal Family's annual holiday at Balmoral in August provides much needed relaxation.

Below right, the Trooping the Colour ceremony is over for another year and the members of the Royal Family stand on the balcony at Buckingham Palace, waving to the crowds in the Mall outside. Prince Philip is on the Queen's left, Prince Edward on her right. Prince Charles stands behind the Queen.

taken after the Trooping the Colour ceremony in 1972. The Queen wears a black arm band as a sign of mourning for her uncle, the Duke of Windsor, formerly King Edward VIII, who had recently died in Paris. A special lament for him was played at the ceremony.

The Private Face

For royalty, a really 'private' private life is anything from difficult to downright impossible. Family tragedies, such as the murder of Lord Mountbatten in 1979, or anxieties such as the emergency operation on the Queen Mother to remove a fishbone from her throat in 1982, inevitably hit the headlines and the Royal Family must spend their more sombre moments in the public eye.

This is why the Queen so greatly values the times when she can 'get away from it all' — the quiet weekends at Windsor, the long summer-into-autumn holiday at Balmoral (interrupted only to attend the Highland Games in September) and the family Christmases spent at Sandringham. On these occasions, the Queen, who is close to all members of her family, can enjoy off-duty time in their company. She takes immense pride and joy in her children and grandchildren — Princess Anne's son Peter (born 1977) and daughter Zara (born 1981) and Prince Charles' son Prince William (born 1982).

There's time, too, for the Queen's personal interests, in which animals figure prominently. She owns several Corgis and Labrador dogs and is an acknowledged expert on horse breeding. She owns and breeds race- and event horses and Fell and Highland ponies and is an excellent horsewoman herself. This was amply demonstrated in 1981 when she calmed her mount Burmese who was frightened by a blank fired with a dummy pistol by a young spectator at the Trooping the Colour. The Queen is always a keen spectator at the Badminton Horse Trials and at events in which Princess Anne and her husband Captain Mark Phillips participate.

The Queen also takes close interest in the Royal Stamp Collection, created by her grandfather King George V, and carefully scrutinises all new British stamp issues sent to her for her approval.

Above, the Queen off duty, laughing happily, standing at the deck rail of the Royal Yacht, Britannia. Right, one of the royal corgis upstaged by four of the Queen's black labradors, but they too get their turn, far right, in this study of the Queen sitting by a tumbling waterfall among the lovely mountainscape near Balmoral Castle in Aberdeenshire in 1972.

Top left, the Queen as a mother, seen here with her two younger children, Prince Andrew and baby Prince Edward. The Queen is very fond of children and always wanted to have a large family but public duties put a gap of ten years between her two elder children, Prince Charles and Princess Anne, and her two younger children. Right, at Balmoral Castle, where the Queen spends her summer holidays enjoying Scottish country pursuits, she is seen smiling at an apparently bashful horse after a morning ride. Below left, the Queen, Prince Philip and their four children in 1964 at the Royal Lodge, Windsor, which can be seen in the background. Below centre, the Queen and her Private Secretary, Sir Martin Charteris, scan official papers on board the Royal Yacht in 1972. Bottom right, the Queen and Prince Philip with a few of the thousands of congratulations they received from all over the world for their Silver Wedding in 1972.

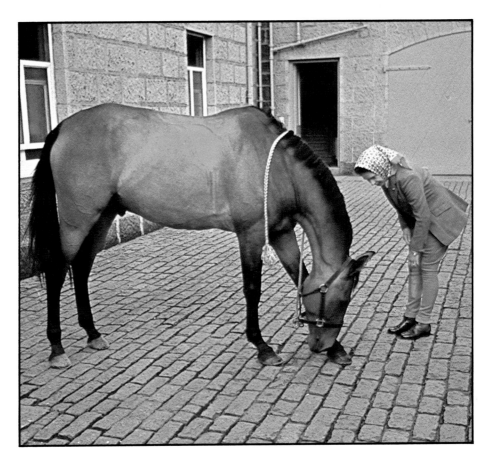

Above, Derby Day in the brilliant summer of 1983 saw the Royal Family out in force for a day at the races. Prince Philip, centre, chats with Princess Anne, who wears a yellow hat and coat, with the Queen on the right and the Queen Mother, in a lilac outfit, on the left. Right, the Queen has always been a keen photographer and has often wielded the camera on her state visits abroad. Here, she awaits the right moment to get the picture she wants at the Windsor Horse Show in the summer of 1982.

Top right, on a visit to a
Zambian game park, the Queen
looks away for a moment as she
stands beside her son, Prince
Andrew. Andrew and his father,
Prince Philip, have obviously
seen something interesting ahead.
On official royal visits overseas,
the Queen has travelled to most
countries of the world. It is rare,
however, in the midst of their
busy programme, that the Queen
and Prince Philip are able to
relax and enjoy the sights and
sounds experienced by other
visitors. Both the Queen and
Prince Philip keep themselves
very well informed about world
affairs and take a keen interest in
all the places they visit.
Below right, the Queen,
informally dressed in scarf,
skirt, blouse and cardigan, at
one of the off-duty open-air
events of which she is so fond.
Once more, she has her camera
with her, ready to bag another
shot for the Royal Family
album. For someone who is
constantly in the camera's eye, it
must be pleasant to be on the
other side of the fence for a
change.

Diana
Princess of Wales

In the very short time since Lady Diana Spencer burst onto the royal scene, to be greeted so wholeheartedly by the British public and the world at large, she has become, as Princess of Wales, a stunning success in the especially tricky role modern royalty has to play. She is, what is more, the world's number one cover girl — her picture on the front of any magazine anywhere, makes it an instant sell out — and so popular on royal walkabouts that crowds have been known to look visibly disappointed if she isn't allocated their side of the street. ''I haven't yet worked out a way of dividing my wife into two,'' Charles confessed ruefully on one such occasion. Diana's very individual style of dress and her low-heeled shoes have turned fashion around, as has the easy, swinging cut she has to her beautiful blonde hair. Princess Diana has certainly revived a role which royalty once played automatically: setting the pace for others to follow. At the same time she has performed remarkably well at the more formal occasion bringing to it an easy, relaxed and warm-hearted style all her own.

The year 1983 saw Diana's first official 'grand' tour, to Australasia, with her husband and baby son, and it was a resounding triumph soon to be followed by her 'conquest' of Canada.

From the somewhat chubby and shy 19-year-old who became engaged to Prince Charles on 24th February 1981, Diana has grown rapidly into an elegant and beautiful young wife and mother and if, as is patently clear, the whole world has fallen in love with her, it is not really the least bit surprising.

Below, the traditional royal appearance on the balcony at Buckingham Palace. Charles and Diana, with bridesmaids and pages, flanked by the Queen, Prince Edward and Prince Andrew on the left. On the right, the Queen Mother and Prince Philip.

Right, the unforgettable Royal Wedding Day, 29th July 1981. The newly married Prince and Princess of Wales descend the steps of St. Paul's Cathedral after a wedding service that was televised around the globe and watched by a record number of viewers before or since.

Previous page, awaiting the happy event, Princess Diana continued to be seen in public until a few days before the birth of Prince William on 21st June 1982. Left, in March 1982, she attended the opening of the Barbican Arts Centre and far left, got away from it all in the Scilly Isles.

Below, Royal Christening day, 4th August, was also the 82nd birthday of the baby's great grandmother, the Queen Mother. The proud parents, with their six-week-old son, William Arthur Philip Louis, are seen after the private, non-televised ceremony at Buckingham Palace.

In the Public Eye

Above, in Autumn 1983 there was speculation about a second royal baby. "How's your baby?" asked Fiona Pasmore when she met the Princess in September. But the Princess only laughed. Below, Royals on show at official occasions wear eye-catching but not overwhelming outfits, an apt description of Diana wearing creamy dress and broad-brimmed boater to ride with the Queen Mother in an open landau at the Trooping the Colour ceremony in 1983.

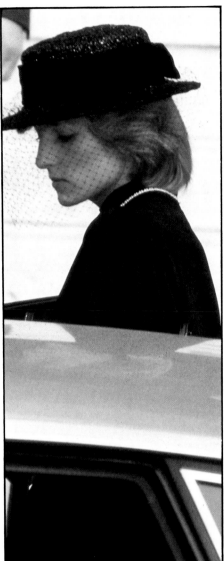

Top right, Princess mourns Princess. Diana represented the Queen at the funeral of Princess Grace of Monaco in September 1982. Diana met Grace only once, on her first public appearance as Charles' fiancée in March 1981.

Above, Diana neat and sweet in a beige plaid coat and beret with black velvet trimmings and a single flower. Left, brilliant pink with ruffles in the suit she wore to brighten the Christmas Day service the Royal Family attended at Windsor in 1982. Right (centre), glamorous and scintillating off-one-shoulder gown for the première of the James Bond film 'Octopussy'. Below right, bright crimson for a ruffle-shouldered coat and hat worn on a visit to Liverpool.

Ambassadress for Britain

The royals arrived in Australia informally, touching down at breakfast time in their Royal Australian Air Force 707 at Alice Springs. It was the start of the Princess of Wales' first — and hugely successful — overseas tour. The recently elected Labour government in Australia had been talking about making the country a republic, but the joyous and enthusiastic welcome the royals received soon altered opinion. Baby Prince William, seen with his parents (left) and with the Princess (top right), stayed with nanny Barbara Barnes at Woomargama, while his parents undertook a hectic programme. At every break in their tour, they returned to Woomargama to relax and be with their baby son. Below left, Charles and Diana meet the children of Alice Springs. Still informal, they sat on the grass for a heart-to-heart chat with them. Below centre, bowling down the street in Perth by Land-Rover, past flag-waving cheering crowds. Below right, out and about in Perth, where the Princess can be seen about to receive a bunch of flowers from the children whose company she so obviously enjoys. It's one of the most heartwarming qualities about the girl who has become the 'People's Princess' in only two short years.

Top left, Prince Charles takes his turn to hold the baby. Below right and left, the Prince and Princess of Wales visit one of Australia's great tourist attractions: the mysterious Ayers Rock, a pair of quartite monoliths in the Northern Territory. They walked part way up the slope of the 1,000-foot-high Rock.

Top left and this page, ten-month-old Prince William of Wales, a large lad for his age, goes crawlabout for the cameras on the lawn of Government House, Auckland, New Zealand's largest city. William performed beautifully for the world's press, crawling, chuckling, smiling and, holding onto father's knee, standing up for the pictures that went round the globe on television screens and magazine covers. The super-sensitive TV microphones also present overheard Prince Charles whisper his son's nickname to him: it was 'Wills'.

Above left, the Prince and Princess seen garlanded, Maori style at Eden Park, Auckland, in New Zealand where they were greeted by a huge crowd of 35,000 delighted, excited and enthusiastic children. Above right, Diana at a rainy Anzac Day Ceremony in Auckland. Below right, the royal couple flanked by Maoris in costume at Auckland. Far right, the Princess, stunning in glittering tiara and another of her sensational evening gowns at a banquet in Auckland. The royal

Top left and this page, ten-month-old Prince William of Wales, a large lad for his age, goes crawlabout for the cameras on the lawn of Government House, Auckland, New Zealand's largest city. William performed beautifully for the world's press, crawling, chuckling, smiling and, holding onto father's knee, standing up for the pictures that went round the globe on television screens and magazine covers. The super-sensitive TV microphones also present overheard Prince Charles whisper his son's nickname to him: it was 'Wills'.

Far left, Diana's bright and easy to wear yellow dress came out often as her answer to keeping and looking cool in Australia's hot weather. The temperature at times scaled as much as 100°F! This picture was taken at Alice Springs. Left (top), Diana's lavishly frilled and candy floss-sparkling blue evening gown created a sensation on a night out dancing in Sydney. Her super slim figure was emphasised by the wide silver belt around her waist. Left (below), out and about in Sydney, with the famous Opera House in the background seemingly engulfed by the enormous welcoming crowd. Right, a quiet, more pensive moment as Diana examines the bouquet on her lap, one of the dozens she received on her tour of Australasia. This picture was taken at Newcastle, where the Princess wore a pink puff-sleeved outfit and the small curly brimmed hat that has become her trademark. Her designer, however, has admitted that all too often, Diana wears his hats the wrong way round, and he now provides her with diagrams and directional arrows so that she can get it right! Whichever way, they look good.

Above left, the Prince and Princess seen garlanded, Maori style at Eden Park, Auckland, in New Zealand where they were *greeted by a huge crowd of 35,000 delighted, excited and enthusiastic children. Above right, Diana at a rainy Anzac* *Day Ceremony in Auckland. Below right, the royal couple flanked by Maoris in costume at Auckland. Far right, the* *Princess, stunning in glittering tiara and another of her sensational evening gowns at a banquet in Auckland. The royal*

pair were reunited with Charles' youngest brother, Prince Edward, who has been teaching at Wanganui College in New Zealand and met them spectacularly clad in a Maori cloak. In New Zealand, the Princess of Wales developed a sore nose from exchanging hundreds of 'hongi' — nose-rubbing — greetings traditional among the Maoris. Top, another picture of Princess Diana, with Charles in a somewhat serious mood, at Newcastle, in Australia.

Above: the Prince and Princess of Wales take a ride on board a 100-foot Maori war canoe at Waitangi, where a crowd of 500 Maoris welcomed them. The senior Maori, left of the picture, wears the traditional cloak similar to Prince Edward's. Right, Charles and Diana attend the farewell banquet in Auckland at the end of their Australasian tour, which also took in Tasmania.
It had been hard going and the couple enjoyed a rest day before flying to Tahiti, Los Angeles and on for a short break in the Bahamas. Prince William went straight home to London with his nanny.

Above, Prince Charles, Princess Diana and Prince Edward — minus his Maori cloak this time — are seen together at Wanganui. Below, yet another cheerful Maori greeting for Diana, this time by 500 Maoris at Gisbourne. Diana was definitely the smash hit success of the Australasian visit and showed how much she has learned about the graceful art of being a touring royal. Once again, though, Prince Charles has been driven by his wife's enormous popularity to contemplate some desperate measures: "Perhaps," he said, "it would be better to have two wives. Then, they could walk down each side of the street, while I stay in the centre directing operations." Behind the lighthearted humour lies the true appreciation the Prince of Wales must feel for the enormous amount of help and support Diana gives him on occasions such as these. With her friendly and lively manner, the Princess is seldom at a loss for words and seems to find the time for a word with everyone she meets.

A few short weeks separated the Australasian tour and the shorter, but no less intensive tour of Canada by the Prince and Princess of Wales. This time, they had to leave Prince William at home and missed his first birthday on 21st June. Diana celebrated her own 22nd birthday in Canada on 1st July, the day before she and Charles returned to England. Top left, the Canadian maple leaf flag is much in evidence as Diana meets the people in Ottawa. Top right, the red-clad Princess, sporting an eye-catching long white collar, with a red-coated Mountie as she arrives in Edmonton, where Prince Charles opened the World University Games.

Far left, heap big welcome for the fascinated Princess from Canadian Indians in feathered head-dresses at St. John's, Newfoundland where the quatercentenary of the first English colony in the New World was celebrated in 1983. Above left, on the second day of her tour, the Princess is seen attending a Youth Rally at St. John's. Left, the Princess, in full-sleeved candy stripe dress meeting children in Ottowa. Canadian P.M. Pierre Trudeau stands to the left of the picture, not quite as attentive as in the picture top left, on the previous page. Top, a royal night out in Halifax, Nova Scotia, where once again Diana caught all eyes.

Back to the days of the old Canadian West, with Prince Charles sporting the same sort of frock coat and suit as his great-great grandfather, King Edward VII, when he visited Canada as Prince of Wales in 1860. Diana, wearing Victorian bustle and tip-tilted bow-trimmed bonnet, was emulating Princess Margaret, who wore Klondike costume when she came to Canada in 1980. The turn-the-clock-back occasion was the Klondike Party held at Fort Edmonton, Alberta, where a barbecue was followed by renderings of music hall favourites, and the informal sing-song was marked by the royal pair linking arms with the other 850 guests. A ride on the open-top Victorian carriage (top left) was all part of the fun, and the wooden walkway on which the royal couple stand (right) was all part of the atmosphere.

The Princess of Wales

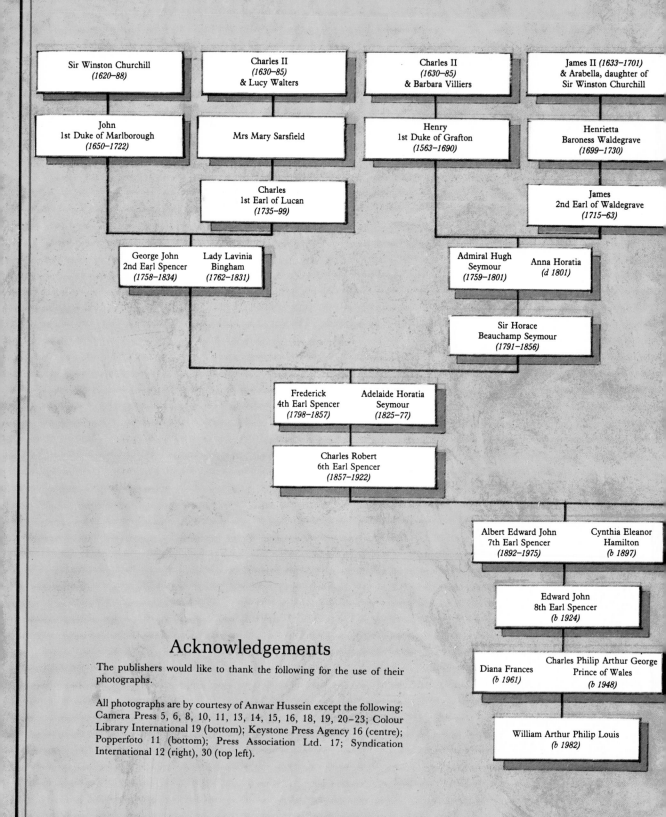

Sir Winston Churchill
(1620–88)

Charles II
(1630–85)
& Lucy Walters

Charles II
(1630–85)
& Barbara Villiers

James II *(1633–1701)*
& Arabella, daughter of
Sir Winston Churchill

John
1st Duke of Marlborough
(1650–1722)

Mrs Mary Sarsfield

Henry
1st Duke of Grafton
(1563–1690)

Henrietta
Baroness Waldegrave
(1699–1730)

Charles
1st Earl of Lucan
(1735–99)

James
2nd Earl of Waldegrave
(1715–63)

George John
2nd Earl Spencer
(1758–1834)

Lady Lavinia
Bingham
(1762–1831)

Admiral Hugh
Seymour
(1759–1801)

Anna Horatia
(d 1801)

Sir Horace
Beauchamp Seymour
(1791–1856)

Frederick
4th Earl Spencer
(1798–1857)

Adelaide Horatia
Seymour
(1825–77)

Charles Robert
6th Earl Spencer
(1857–1922)

Albert Edward John
7th Earl Spencer
(1892–1975)

Cynthia Eleanor
Hamilton
(b 1897)

Edward John
8th Earl Spencer
(b 1924)

Diana Frances
(b 1961)

Charles Philip Arthur George
Prince of Wales
(b 1948)

William Arthur Philip Louis
(b 1982)

Acknowledgements

The publishers would like to thank the following for the use of their photographs.

All photographs are by courtesy of Anwar Hussein except the following: Camera Press 5, 6, 8, 10, 11, 13, 14, 15, 16, 18, 19, 20–23; Colour Library International 19 (bottom); Keystone Press Agency 16 (centre); Popperfoto 11 (bottom); Press Association Ltd. 17; Syndication International 12 (right), 30 (top left).